2018 SQA Specimen Past Papers with Answers

National 5 BUSINESS MANAGEMENT

2016, 2017 & 2018 Exams
and 2017 Specimen Question Paper

HODDER
GIBSON
AN HACHETTE UK COMPANY

This book contains the official SQA 2016, 2017 and 2018 Exams, and the 2017 Specimen Question Paper for National 5 Business Management, with associated SQA-approved answers modified from the official marking instructions that accompany the paper.

In addition the book contains study skills advice. This has been specially commissioned by Hodder Gibson, and has been written by experienced senior teachers and examiners in line with the new National 5 syllabus and assessment outlines. This is not SQA material but has been devised to provide further guidance for National 5 examinations.

Hodder Gibson is grateful to the copyright holders, as credited on the final page of the book, for permission to use their material. Every effort has been made to trace the copyright holders and to obtain their permission for the use of copyright material. Hodder Gibson will be happy to receive information allowing us to rectify any error or omission in future editions.

Hachette UK's policy is to use papers that are natural, renewable and recyclable products and made from wood grown in sustainable forests. The logging and manufacturing processes are expected to conform to the environmental regulations of the country of origin.

Orders: please contact Bookpoint Ltd, 130 Park Drive, Milton Park, Abingdon, Oxon OX14 4SE. Telephone: (44) 01235 827827. Fax: (44) 01235 400454. Lines are open 9.00–5.00, Monday to Saturday, with a 24-hour message answering service. Visit our website at www.hoddereducation.co.uk. Hodder Gibson can also be contacted directly at hoddergibson@hodder.co.uk

This collection first published in 2018 by
Hodder Gibson, an imprint of Hodder Education,
An Hachette UK Company
211 St Vincent Street
Glasgow G2 5QY

Typeset by Aptara, Inc.

Printed in the UK

A catalogue record for this title is available from the British Library

ISBN: 978-1-5104-5660-0

2 1

2019 2018

Introduction

National 5 Business Management

This book of SQA past papers contains the question papers used in the 2016, 2017 and 2018 exams (with answers at the back of the book). A specimen question paper reflecting the content and duration of the exam in 2018 is also included.

All of the question papers included in the book provide excellent representative exam practice for the final exams. Using these papers as part of your revision will help you to develop the vital skills and techniques needed for the exam, and will help you identify any knowledge gaps you may have.

It is always a very good idea to refer to SQA's website for the most up-to-date course specification documents. These are available at www.sqa.org.uk/sqa/47436

The course

The National 5 Business Management course should enable you to develop:

- knowledge and understanding of the ways in which society relies on business to satisfy our needs
- an insight into the systems that organisations use to ensure customers' needs are met
- enterprising skills and attributes by providing you with opportunities to explore realistic business situations
- financial awareness through business contexts
- an insight into how organisations organise their resources for maximum efficiency and to improve their overall performance
- an awareness of how external influences impact on organisations.

The course is split into the following areas of study. The final exam can include questions on any of these areas.

- Understanding business
- Management of marketing
- Management of operations
- Management of people
- Management of finance

How the course is graded

The grade you achieve at the end of the National 5 Business Management course depends on two assessments:

- Assignment – this is submitted to SQA before your exam and counts for 25% of your final grade
- Exam – this counts for 75% of your final grade.

The course assessment for Session 2017/18 onwards

Question Paper

The Question Paper is now worth 90 marks (previously 70 marks) and contributes to 75% of your overall grade awarded for the Course.

Section 1 comprises 40 marks in total. This is made up of two pieces of stimulus material and questions of 20 marks each. The stimulus may be in the form of text, diagrams, financial information or graphs. The questions will be associated with the stimulus material and you should try, where possible, to relate your answers to the material provided. It will be based on real organisations. The questions can be drawn from any area of the course and will focus on decision making and the application of knowledge and understanding. Each question is broken down into sub-questions and the marks for each sub-question will range between 1–5 marks.

Section 2 comprises 50 marks in total. This is made up of five questions of 10 marks each. The questions can be drawn from any area of the course and will focus on the application of knowledge and understanding. The marks for each question in Section 2 will range between 1–4 marks.

You must attempt all questions in the question paper and it must be completed within 2 hours. The question paper is marked by SQA.

Assignment

The Assignment is worth 30 marks and contributes to 25% of your overall grade awarded for the Course.

The assignment gives you the opportunity to demonstrate your ability to:

- select an appropriate business topic.
- research and gather suitable business data/information/evidence relating to the context of the topic, from a range of sources.
- apply knowledge and understanding of business concepts to explain and analyse the key features of the topic.
- draw valid conclusions and/or recommendations to make informed business judgements and/or decisions.
- produce an appropriately formatted business report suitable for the purpose, intended audience and context of the assignment.

You will be given up to 5 hours in which to research and write up your final report before submitting it to SQA for marking. You must complete the assignment on your own, although your teacher will be able to give you some assistance in line with the guidance provided by SQA. This is an opportunity for you to gain valuable marks for your own piece of work.

Marks for the assignment are awarded for the following areas:

- background information – 4 marks
- research methods and sources – 6 marks
- findings, analysis and interpretation – 12 marks
- conclusion(s)/recommendation(s) – 6 marks
- collating and reporting – 2 marks

Your final report should be no longer than 1,300 words (excluding appendices). If the word count exceeds the maximum by more than 10%, a penalty will be applied when it is marked. There should be no more than two pages of appendices attached to your report.

Command words

It is often the case that candidates in the exam misunderstand what the question is asking them as they don't realise the importance of what is called the "Command Word". For example, if a question asks you to **identify** something, you only need to say what it is. However, if the question asks you to **describe** it, then you need to give some of the main features.

Example 1

Question: *Identify* a source of finance for a business.

1 mark

Acceptable answer: *A source of finance could be a Bank Loan.*

This answer will receive a mark as it does what the command word **identify** has asked.

Example 2

Question: *Describe* a source of finance for a business.

1 mark

Acceptable answer: *A loan from a bank which can be repaid with interest, over a period of time.*

In this case, where the command word is **describe**, there would be no marks awarded for the answer given in Example 1. You need to include some features of a bank loan (describe it) in order to get the mark. Remember, it is good practice to always answer in sentences.

So make sure you read the question carefully, checking the command word to see how you need to write your answer.

Context

Section 1 questions in the exam will provide you with a short piece of stimulus material, sometimes called a case study, with information about a small or medium sized business. The questions that follow will mostly relate to the case study and your answers should reflect the context given.

For example, if the case study is about a charity, then your answers should relate to a charity.

Example 3

Question: *Give* an objective for the RSPCA. *1 mark*

Acceptable answer: *To promote animal welfare.*

Because the RSPCA is a charity there are a number of objectives that would not be suitable for them. For example, you would get no marks for saying an objective would be to make as much profit as possible.

Remember to relate all your answers to the business or organisation from the case study.

Marks

Check the number of marks for each question. Too often candidates write too much or too little. If there is only one mark available then you only need to make one point. It might be safer to give two just in case, but only if you have time. If there are four marks available, then you need to make four points to get full marks.

Check to make sure that you have made enough points in your answer to get full marks.

Topic areas

Understanding Business and Marketing are areas where candidates normally do well in exams. However, Finance proves tricky for a lot of students, and, to a lesser extent, so do Human Resources and Operations. There is no way to avoid questions on these topics, so you will need to learn what is contained in each.

Management of finance

There are only five parts to finance: sources of finance, break-even, cash budgeting, income statement and technology.

For sources of finance you only need to be aware of where the organisation can get money from. Remember, this can be either to invest in the business or to overcome a cash flow problem, so make sure you understand which you should write about, as the acceptable answers may be different for different questions.

For break-even, you need to memorise the formula for calculating contribution and break-even. Once you have done this, these questions should be fairly straightforward. Don't be put off by the use of numbers. The calculations you may be asked to carry out are relatively simple and you will be able to use a calculator.

When looking at cash budgets in a question, it is always better to read left to right rather than up and down. Look for trends, such as a source of income going down, or a cost that is increasing. These would show potential problems which the business should worry about.

Management of people

Candidates often confuse what is included under each heading for recruitment and selection.

- **Recruitment**

  It is generally accepted that the recruitment stage involves job analysis, job description, person specification, the decision about whether to recruit internally or externally, and, finally, the advertisement of the job.

- **Selection**

  Here you will be expected to give answers about selection methods. These could include application forms/CVs, references, interviews and the various forms of testing available.

  Remember that the recruitment stage is about the job and the selection stage is about picking the right person!

Management of operations

The main problem encountered by candidates is what is meant by quality. There are only two methods you need to know about.

- **Quality control**

  This is a simple system where the quality of raw materials is checked at the start of production, and the quality of the finished product is checked at the end.

- **Quality management**

  Here quality is checked at every stage from carrying out market research to learn what the customers need from the product, to providing quality after-sales service.

Problem answers

Some of the answers you might give to a question are not suitable for gaining marks. Try not to use answers such as "quicker", "easier", "more efficient", "saves time", "saves money" as these do not attract marks. They are *relative terms* and if you do use them you must show what you are comparing them to.

Example 4

Question: _Outline_ *an advantage of using spreadsheets in Finance.*   ***1 mark***

Acceptable answer: *Formulas in the spreadsheet will carry out calculations automatically.*

You would not get a mark for saying it is faster than doing calculations by hand.

Always use business terminology in your answers – this is far more likely to get you the marks!

Good luck!

A lot of what you will learn in National 5 Business Management is common sense. As a consumer and a member of society you are already aware of most of the course content. The challenge is to make sure you understand the terms used. Hard work and good preparation go a long way, so keep calm and don't panic! GOOD LUCK!

Study Skills – what you need to know to pass exams!

General exam revision: 20 top tips

When preparing for exams, it is easy to feel unsure of where to start or how to revise. This guide to general exam revision provides a good starting place, and, as these are very general tips, they can be applied to all your exams.

1. Start revising in good time.

Don't leave revision until the last minute – this will make you panic and it will be difficult to learn. Make a revision timetable that counts down the weeks to go.

2. Work to a study plan.

Set up sessions of work spread through the weeks ahead. Make sure each session has a focus and a clear purpose. What will you study, when and why? Be realistic about what you can achieve in each session, and don't be afraid to adjust your plans as needed.

3. Make sure you know exactly when your exams are.

Get your exam dates from the SQA website and use the timetable builder tool to create your own exam schedule. You will also get a personalised timetable from your school, but this might not be until close to the exam period.

4. Make sure that you know the topics that make up each course.

Studying is easier if material is in manageable chunks – why not use the SQA topic headings or create your own from your class notes? Ask your teacher for help on this if you are not sure.

5. Break the chunks up into even smaller bits.

The small chunks should be easier to cope with. Remember that they fit together to make larger ideas. Even the process of chunking down will help!

6. Ask yourself these key questions for each course:

- Are all topics compulsory or are there choices?
- Which topics seem to come up time and time again?
- Which topics are your strongest and which are your weakest?

Use your answers to these questions to work out how much time you will need to spend revising each topic.

7. Make sure you know what to expect in the exam.

The subject-specific introduction to this book will help with this. Make sure you can answer these questions:

- How is the paper structured?
- How much time is there for each part of the exam?
- What types of question are involved? These will vary depending on the subject so read the subject-specific section carefully.

8. Past papers are a vital revision tool!

Use past papers to support your revision wherever possible. This book contains the answers and mark schemes too – refer to these carefully when checking your work. Using the mark scheme is useful; even if you don't manage to get all the marks available first time when you first practise, it helps you identify how to extend and develop your answers to get more marks next time – and of course, in the real exam.

9. Use study methods that work well for you.

People study and learn in different ways. Reading and looking at diagrams suits some students. Others prefer to listen and hear material – what about reading out loud or getting a friend or family member to do this for you? You could also record and play back material.

10. There are three tried and tested ways to make material stick in your long-term memory:

- Practising – e.g. rehearsal, repeating
- Organising – e.g. making drawings, lists, diagrams, tables, memory aids
- Elaborating – e.g. incorporating the material into a story or an imagined journey

11. Learn actively.

Most people prefer to learn actively – for example, making notes, highlighting, redrawing and redrafting, making up memory aids, or writing past paper answers. A good way to stay engaged and inspired is to mix and match these methods – find the combination that best suits you. This is likely to vary depending on the topic or subject.

12. Be an expert.

Be sure to have a few areas in which you feel you are an expert. This often works because at least some of them will come up, which can boost confidence.

13. Try some visual methods.

Use symbols, diagrams, charts, flashcards, post-it notes etc. Don't forget – the brain takes in chunked images more easily than loads of text.

14. Remember – practice makes perfect.

Work on difficult areas again and again. Look and read – then test yourself. You cannot do this too much.

15. Try past papers against the clock.

Practise writing answers in a set time. This is a good habit from the start but is especially important when you get closer to exam time.

16. Collaborate with friends.

Test each other and talk about the material – this can really help. Two brains are better than one! It is amazing how talking about a problem can help you solve it.

17. Know your weaknesses.

Ask your teacher for help to identify what you don't know. Try to do this as early as possible. If you are having trouble, it is probably with a difficult topic, so your teacher will already be aware of this – most students will find it tough.

18. Have your materials organised and ready.

Know what is needed for each exam:

- Do you need a calculator or a ruler?
- Should you have pencils as well as pens?
- Will you need water or paper tissues?

19. Make full use of school resources.

Find out what support is on offer:

- Are there study classes available?
- When is the library open?
- When is the best time to ask for extra help?
- Can you borrow textbooks, study guides, past papers, etc.?
- Is school open for Easter revision?

20. Keep fit and healthy!

Try to stick to a routine as much as possible, including with sleep. If you are tired, sluggish or dehydrated, it is difficult to see how concentration is even possible. Combine study with relaxation, drink plenty of water, eat sensibly, and get fresh air and exercise – all these things will help more than you could imagine. Good luck!

NATIONAL 5

2016

National Qualifications 2016

X710/75/11

Business Management

FRIDAY, 27 MAY

9:00 AM — 10:30 AM

Total marks — 70

SECTION 1 — 30 marks

Attempt BOTH questions.

SECTION 2 — 40 marks

Attempt ALL questions.

Write your answers clearly in the answer booklet provided. In the answer booklet you must clearly identify the question number you are attempting.

Use **blue** or **black** ink.

You may use a calculator.

Before leaving the examination room you must give your answer booklet to the Invigilator; if you do not, you may lose all the marks for this paper.

MARKS

SECTION 1 — 30 marks

Attempt BOTH questions

Question 1 of this paper replaces the original one in the SQA Past Paper 2016, which cannot be reproduced for copyright reasons. As such, it should be stressed that it is not an official SQA-verified section, although every care has been taken by the Publishers to ensure that it offers appropriate practice material for National 5 Business Management.

Just Dogs

Just Dogs was established in December 2006 by Gemma Johnstone. As a devoted dog owner and dog lover Gemma wanted to offer "doggy" people the chance to visit a shop that would offer a great selection of quality and unique dog accessories and supplies. Whilst the online doggy market proves popular, Gemma wanted to give dog owners the opportunity to be able to visit the shop, see the products and try them out before purchasing. Gemma also likes to be on hand to offer advice and tips to customers who visit the shop, which is based in Edinburgh.

Gemma is currently studying towards the Advanced Diploma in Canine Behaviour. This means that she is able to provide competent advice regarding dog training, behaviour and nutrition. It is important to Gemma to be able to offer a personal, tailored service to customers and this is central to the way the business is operated.

Just Dogs promotes responsible dog ownership. All of its practical doggy products are accompanied with useful guidance, tips and messages. This allows owners to look after their dogs in the best possible manner.

Adapted from www.justdogsshop.co.uk

You should note that although the following questions are based on the case study above, you will need to make use of knowledge and understanding you have gained whilst studying the Course.

1. (a) (i) From the case study, identify the type of business that Gemma operates.   1

   (ii) Using information from the case study and knowledge that you have gained, give 2 examples of good customer service.   2

   (b) Describe 2 costs and 2 benefits to Gemma of operating a website as well as her shop.   4

   (c) Outline methods of promotion that Gemma could use for her business.   3

   (d) Gemma is undertaking training to help her provide a better service to her customers.

   Describe the benefits of staff training.   3

   (e) Describe 2 costs that Gemma may have in her business.   2

MARKS

WHO MADE YOUR PANTS?

Who Made Your Pants? is an ethical business that was launched in 2008 by Becky John because she really didn't like wearing clothes that were made in sweatshop conditions. The company makes underwear using traditional fabrics, like lycra and lace, which are bought from big underwear companies. These fabrics are unwanted materials which are normally thrown out as waste at the end of a season.

In 2014, Becky won Social Entrepreneur of the Year for her business that creates manufacturing jobs for women who have been excluded due to their status as refugees. She employs 8 women with refugee backgrounds from countries such as Sudan, Somalia and Afghanistan.

The company provides training and every new recruit starts by working on one style of underwear and then moves onto the more complicated styles. The pants are handmade and each woman has a specialist job like cutting, sewing or trimming so there will always be more than one person involved in the making of each piece of underwear. All profits the company makes go back into the business.

You should note that although the following questions are based on the case study above, you will need to make use of knowledge and understanding you have gained whilst studying the Course.

2. (a) (i) From the case study, identify **one** way that Who Made Your Pants is ethical in its production. 1

(ii) Justify the importance of ethical production. 3

(b) Who Made Your Pants sells its products online.

Explain the benefits of online selling (e-commerce). 3

(c) (i) Identify **one** type of training used by Who Made Your Pants. 1

(ii) Describe an advantage of the type of training identified in (c)(i). 1

(d) Describe the methods of selection that could be used by Who Made Your Pants. 3

(e) Describe the methods that Who Made Your Pants could use to ensure the quality of its underwear. 3

[Turn over

MARKS

SECTION 2 — 40 marks

Attempt ALL questions

3. (a) Internal factors can influence performance.

        (i) Identify **2** internal factors.   2

        (ii) Explain the influence of the factors identified in (a)(i).   2

    (b) Outline the objectives of a non-profit-making organisation.   2

provide — — help a specific cause

    (c) Discuss the advantages and disadvantages of operating as a sole trader.   4

4. (a) Outline the ways an organisation could use the following technology in the recruitment and selection process.

        (i) Word processing package   1

        (ii) Database package   1

        (iii) Company website   1

    (b) (i) Identify **2** methods of industrial action.   2

        (ii) Explain the impact of industrial action.   3

    (c) Outline the impact of technology on working practices.   2

[Turn over

MARKS

5. **Cash Budget for Green Energy Solutions Ltd**

	£	£	£
	May	June	July
OPENING BALANCE	20,000	(3,000)	(2,000)
RECEIPTS			
Sales Revenue	2,000	8,000	13,000
TOTAL	22,000	5,000	11,000
PAYMENTS			
Purchases	1,000	2,000	3,500
Wages	3,000	4,000	4,000
Advertising	1,000	1,000	1,000
Purchase of Motor Van	20,000	0	0
TOTAL	25,000	7,000	8,500
CLOSING BALANCE	**(3,000)**	**(2,000)**	**2,500**

(a) (i) From the cash budget, identify **2** cash flow problems. 2

(ii) Describe how the problems identified in part (a)(i) could be solved. 4

(b) From the cash budget, identify an example of:

(i) a fixed cost; 1

(ii) a variable cost. 1

(c) Outline the purposes of producing an income statement. 2

6. (a) Describe the methods of production. 3

(b) Outline the factors an organisation might consider when choosing a supplier. 3

(c) Explain the possible problems of:

- under-stocking;

- over-stocking. 4

[END OF QUESTION PAPER]

[BLANK PAGE]

DO NOT WRITE ON THIS PAGE

NATIONAL 5

2017

National Qualifications 2017

X710/75/11

Business Management

TUESDAY, 16 MAY

9:00 AM – 10:30 AM

Total marks — 70

SECTION 1 — 30 marks

Attempt BOTH questions.

SECTION 2 — 40 marks

Attempt ALL questions.

Write your answers clearly in the answer booklet provided. In the answer booklet you must clearly identify the question number you are attempting.

Use **blue** or **black** ink.

You may use a calculator.

Before leaving the examination room you must give your answer booklet to the Invigilator; if you do not, you may lose all the marks for this paper.

MARKS

SECTION 1 — 30 marks

Attempt BOTH questions

Charles MacLeod's famous Stornoway Black Pudding can be found on menus in restaurants all over the UK. It has also featured in many restaurant reviews in newspapers. Charles MacLeod Ltd is a family run butcher that prides itself on its customer satisfaction.

The business makes the famous black pudding by hand in its premises on the Isle of Lewis under strict UK health and safety food production regulations. "Stornoway Black Pudding" is a term that is protected by European Union legislation which states it must be made in Stornoway. Rivals therefore cannot use the name "Stornoway" in their brand.

The distinctive MacLeod tartan design makes its shop premises stand out in Stornoway. Due to the high demand for the puddings, the business rarely needs to advertise; however they use a well-designed website and social media to communicate with customers.

You should note that although the following questions are based on the case study above, you will need to make use of knowledge and understanding you have gained whilst studying the Course.

1. (a) (i) From the case study, identify the methods used to promote the business. **2**

    (ii) Explain the benefits of branding to the business. **3**

    (b) (i) State a suitable method that could be used to distribute the products to butchers across the UK. **1**

    (ii) Discuss the costs and benefits of using the method of distribution stated in (b)(i). **3**

    (c) From the case study, describe the effect of external factors on the business. **3**

    (d) Compare the features of a private limited company to a sole trader. **3**

MARKS

The owners of iQ Superfood Chocolate, based in Stirling, have taken advantage of the recent growth in the market for organic foods by introducing a range of healthy chocolate products.

iQ has come up with a delicious chocolate range, which contains super food nutrients and antioxidants. Bars have less than 199 calories with a taste to delight chocolate-lovers and the health-conscious alike. The business has also produced new "BeautiQ" and "YogiQ" bars which it claims are specifically beneficial to the skin and health. iQ is particular to ensure that it, along with its suppliers, plays its part in ethical sourcing and distribution.

The bars can be bought in independent retailers and health centres but the business aims to have these products stocked in all the major retailers in the UK.

You should note that although the following questions are based on the case study above, you will need to make use of knowledge and understanding you have gained whilst studying the Course.

2. (a) (i) From the case study, identify the markets targeted by iQ. 2

 (ii) Outline the benefits of target marketing for a business. 3

 (b) (i) Describe a suitable method of production for making iQ products. 1

 (ii) Discuss the costs and benefits of using the method of production described in (b)(i). 3

 (c) Describe the costs and benefits of having an ethical approach to sourcing and distribution of products. 3

 (d) Explain how stakeholders identified in the case study can influence the business. 3

[Turn over

MARKS

SECTION 2 — 40 marks

Attempt ALL questions

3. (a) (i) Identify **2** sectors of the economy.   **2**

       (ii) Compare the objectives of the sectors identified in (a)(i).   **2**

   (b) Describe **3** methods of ensuring good customer service.   **3**

   (c) Explain how internal factors could influence the success of the organisation.   **3**

4. (a) Describe the documents that could be used in the recruitment process.   **3**

   (b) Compare the use of internal and external methods of recruitment.   **2**

   (c) Explain the benefits of training employees.   **3**

   (d) Outline the features of the Equality Act.   **2**

5. (a) Describe the types of technology which could be used within the operations function.   **4**

   (b) (i) Describe the methods that an organisation could use to ensure the quality of its finished goods.   **4**

       (ii) Define the following terms:

- Maximum inventory (stock) level
- Lead time.   **2**

MARKS

6. John McLean is a sole trader who operates a small business. He has produced the following Income Statement for Year 2.

Income Statement for John McLean For the year ended 31 December Year 2	£	£
A		70,000
Less Cost of Sales		40,000
Gross Profit		B
Less Expenses		
Electricity	1,000	
Rent	4,000	
Wages	5,000	
		10,000
PROFIT FOR THE YEAR		C

(a) From the Income Statement, complete the missing information for entries **A**, **B** and **C**.

3

(b) (i) Describe the sources of finance available to a private limited company for expansion.

2

    (ii) Justify the use of sources of finance outlined in (b)(i). (A different justification should be given for each source.)

3

(c) Outline the benefits of budgeting to an organisation.

2

[END OF QUESTION PAPER]

[BLANK PAGE]

DO NOT WRITE ON THIS PAGE

National Qualifications
SPECIMEN ONLY

S810/75/11

Business Management

Date — Not applicable

Duration — 2 hours

Total marks — 90

SECTION 1 — 40 marks

Attempt BOTH questions.

SECTION 2 — 50 marks

Attempt ALL questions.

Write your answers clearly in the answer booklet provided. In the answer booklet you must clearly identify the question number you are attempting.

Use **blue** or **black** ink.

You may use a calculator.

Before leaving the examination room you must give your answer booklet to the Invigilator; if you do not, you may lose all the marks for this paper.

SECTION 1 — 40 marks

Attempt BOTH questions

Background

Cuddybridge is a small producer of apple juice based in the Scottish Borders. The company began by producing cider in 2007 but soon realised that there was too much competition in the market from large brands and decided it was more profitable to produce apple juice.

CUDDYBRIDGE
Made from apples hand pressed in the Scottish Borders:
APPLE JUICE

Production

All the apples are hand pressed and no artificial flavourings, colourings or E-numbers are added. Cuddybridge tries to press the apples as soon as they are received, so that customers get the freshest juice possible.

The company uses more than 15,000 kilograms of apples per week, 365 days of the year, so relying on Scottish apples alone is not an option. Cuddybridge is aware that importing apples increases its carbon footprint. In order to be environmentally friendly it sends all its waste squashed apples to become animal feed for two types of rare breed pigs.

Cuddybridge's client list continues to increase and it now sells to cafes, delis and restaurants around the Borders. It has also recently started to supply top-named restaurants in Edinburgh as well as the famous department store Harvey Nichols. It has won many awards including Scotland Food and Drink Excellence Awards.

The top three product trends with fast paced growth:

1 Vegetable Nutrition - New products with vegetables as an ingredient have seen 43% growth rate between 2012 and 2015

2 All Natural - 67% of consumers rated "all natural" as the most interesting product attribute

3 Speciality 100% Juice - 60% globally say they are interested in products with proven health benefits

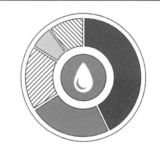

UK soft drinks sectors

- Carbonates (43%)
- Dilutables (23%)
- Bottled water (18%)
- Fruit juice (6%)
- Still and juice drinks (10%)

MARKS

The following questions are based on the case study. You will need to make use of knowledge and understanding you have gained whilst studying the course.

1. (a) (i) From the case study, identify **one** way that Cuddybridge is ethical in its production.　1

(ii) Justify the importance of ethical production.　3

(b) Compare job production with flow production.　3

(c) (i) Using the case study, identify reasons why Cuddybridge started producing apple juice.　2

(ii) Explain how external factors could affect the success of Cuddybridge.　5

(d) Describe methods that Cuddybridge could use to ensure the quality of its apple juice.　3

(e) (i) Identify a suitable method of distribution for Cuddybridge Apple Juice.　1

(ii) Justify the method identified in (e)(i).　2

MARKS

It has been more than 10 years since Jamie Oliver opened his Fifteen restaurant in London as a social enterprise, which was followed on a Channel 4 documentary called Jamie's Kitchen.

Jamie had the vision of creating one of London's finest restaurants and using the magic of cooking to give young people who have faced enormous challenges in their lives the opportunity to unlock their true talent through providing great training and mentoring. The year-long apprenticeship consisted of working alongside top chefs in the restaurant and also spending time at college.

To apply for the apprenticeship applicants had to be between 16 and 24 and not be in employment, education or training. In the first year there were over 300 applications for just 21 places.

All profits from the restaurants are donated to The Jamie Oliver Food Foundation which is a charity that aims to teach people about food, where it comes from, how it affects their bodies and how to cook it.

£1.20

The Daily News

CITY FINAL   Monday 20th February 2017   VOL 32 NO.10

Rising Prices and Shrinking Products

Dispatches, a Channel 4 documentary, reported that after Brexit food prices in the UK were increasing, mainly due to the rising cost of raw materials from Europe. As a result the prices paid by consumers for restaurant meals has also increased.

Source: Channel4Dispatches - Supermarkets: Brexit & Your Shrinking Shop

MARKS

The following questions are based on the case study. You will need to make use of knowledge and understanding you have gained whilst studying the course.

2. (a) (i) From the case study, identify a type of training used by Fifteen. **1**

       (ii) Discuss the advantages and disadvantages of the type of training identified in (a)(i). **3**

(b) Describe methods of selection that could be used by Fifteen to select apprentices. **4**

(c) Using the case study, compare the objectives of Fifteen with those of an organisation in the private sector. **3**

(d) Explain the benefits to Fifteen of Jamie's celebrity endorsement. **3**

(e) Describe how technology could be used in the marketing and operations functions of Fifteen. **3**

(f) Outline ways that Fifteen could reduce costs. **3**

MARKS

SECTION 2 — 50 marks

Attempt ALL questions

3. (a) (i) Identify **2** stakeholders of a private sector organisation.   2

         (ii) Explain the impact that the stakeholders identified in (a)(i) could have on the organisation.   3

   (b) Outline how an organisation could maximise customer satisfaction.   3

   (c) Distinguish between a sole trader and a private limited company.   2

4. (a) (i) Outline the factors that would be considered before setting a price for a product.   3

         (ii) Describe pricing strategies for a new product.   2

   (b) Explain the benefits of branding.   3

   (c) Describe how an organisation can be ethical in its marketing activities.   2

5. (a) Outline the stages of the recruitment process.   4

   (b) Describe payment systems used to calculate employee wages.   4

   (c) Identify **2** pieces of employment legislation.   2

MARKS

6. **Cash Budget for Blooming Florist Ltd**

	£ May	£ June	£ July
OPENING BALANCE	20,000	−3,000	−2,000
RECEIPTS			
Sales Revenue	2,000	(ii)	13,000
TOTAL	22,000	5,000	11,000
PAYMENTS			
Purchases	1,000	2,000	3,500
Wages	3,000	4,000	4,000
Advertising	1,000	1,000	1,000
Purchase of Motor Van	(i)	0	0
TOTAL	25,000	7,000	8,500
CLOSING BALANCE	**−3,000**	**−2,000**	**2,500**

(a) From the cash budget, calculate the missing figures (i) and (ii).   2

(b) Discuss sources of finance that could be used by a private limited company.   4

(c) Justify the use of spreadsheets in the Finance department.   2

(d) Outline the purpose of producing an Income Statement.   2

7. (a) Describe the factors that would be considered before choosing a supplier of raw materials.   4

(b) Draw and label an inventory control diagram.   3

(c) Explain the problems that could be encountered if an organisation:

  • overstocks

  • understocks.   3

[END OF SPECIMEN QUESTION PAPER]

[BLANK PAGE]

DO NOT WRITE ON THIS PAGE

NATIONAL 5

2018

National Qualifications 2018

X810/75/11

Business Management

FRIDAY, 18 MAY

9:00 AM — 11:00 AM

Total marks — 90

SECTION 1 — 40 marks

Attempt BOTH questions.

SECTION 2 — 50 marks

Attempt ALL questions.

Write your answers clearly in the answer booklet provided. In the answer booklet you must clearly identify the question number you are attempting.

Use **blue** or **black** ink.

You may use a calculator.

Before leaving the examination room you must give your answer booklet to the Invigilator; if you do not, you may lose all the marks for this paper.

SECTION 1 — 40 marks

Attempt BOTH questions

HelloFresh, founded in 2011, is a global business that is headquartered in Berlin. It aims to transform the way people cook and eat. HelloFresh delivers recipes and ingredients to your door in a chilled box six days a week. It provides all the ingredients you need to cook a meal, already measured out. All you need to have at home is salt, pepper, olive oil and butter. The recipe cards are designed so that a meal can be prepared and cooked in only 30 minutes.

HelloFresh UK, the UK arm of HelloFresh Group, limits packaging and it sources food from local British suppliers to minimise its carbon footprint. All boxes, bags and spice containers are recyclable. The wool liners, which wrap around chilled ingredients, are great for compost. Some inventive people even use the liners as bedding for pets.

HelloFresh sales revenue has grown from £2 million in 2012 to £304 million in 2015.

There is strong competition in the recipe box delivery sector. In addition to HelloFresh there are a number of other companies that operate in the sector, including Gousto and Weight Watchers Smart Kitchen. The following table shows the cost of 3 meals for 2 people from each of the delivery services:

Company	Price per Box	Introductory Offer
Hello Fresh	£34·99	50% off first box
Gousto	£29·99	50% off first and second box
Weight Watchers Smart Kitchen	£30·00	None

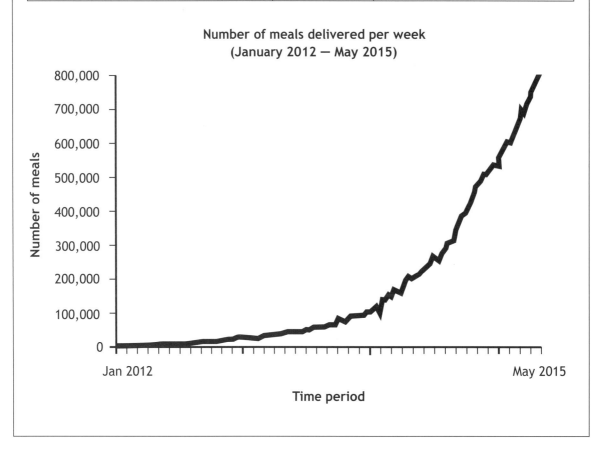

Number of meals delivered per week
(January 2012 — May 2015)

MARKS

The following questions are based on the case study. You will need to make use of knowledge and understanding you have gained whilst studying the course.

1. (a)   (i)   From the case study, outline the steps HelloFresh UK is taking to be environmentally friendly.   **2**

   (ii)   Explain the importance to HelloFresh of being environmentally friendly.   **3**

   (b)   (i)   From the case study, identify the trend in the recipe box delivery sector.   **1**

   (ii)   Describe the external factors that may have led to the trend identified in 1(b)(i).   **2**

   (c)   Describe the factors that may influence HelloFresh in its choice of supplier.   **4**

   (d)   HelloFresh offers an introductory discount to new customers.

   Describe the **other** methods it could use to promote its business.   **3**

   (e)   Describe the sources of finance that HelloFresh could use to expand.   **5**

[Turn over

Children's Hospices Across Scotland

Children's Hospices Across Scotland, better known as (CHAS), is Scotland's national children's hospice service for children and young people who have life-shortening conditions for which there is no known cure. They are dedicated to supporting every single one of these families. They make sure that no matter how short the time a family have together, it is filled with happiness and fun. They help parents to celebrate the lives of their children while they are together, and to honour their memory when they are gone.

CHAS raises funds through fundraising in communities, key partnerships and donations from individuals. It has a website for online donations, as well as a social media presence across multiple sites. It works with over 800 volunteers who help the organisation across their care services and fundraising.

CHAS also has a retail arm which last year brought in over £400,000, mostly from the sale of second hand goods in their shops. They also generate extra income from door-step clothing collection. CHAS aims to get the most from items donated, for example, any items that cannot be sold in CHAS shops are sold to companies who recycle them.

UK charities' statistics

Over 160,000 charities in the UK

UK charities combined income £39 billion per year

44 million people donate on a regular basis

The following questions are based on the case study. You will need to make use of knowledge and understanding you have gained whilst studying the course.

MARKS

2. (a) (i) From the case study, identify the sector of the economy that CHAS operates in. **1**

    (ii) Compare the objectives of the sector identified in 2(a)(i) with one other sector of the economy. **3**

    (b) CHAS has a workforce made up of both employees and volunteers.

    (i) Outline the costs and benefits of staff training. **4**

    (ii) State the methods, other than training, CHAS may use to motivate its workforce. **4**

    (c) Explain the benefits to CHAS of choosing a suitable location for its shops. **3**

    (d) (i) From the case study, identify **2** types of technology used by the marketing function of CHAS. **2**

    (ii) Describe the use of technology in the marketing department of CHAS. **3**

MARKS

SECTION 2 — 50 marks

Attempt ALL questions

3. (a) Describe the use of market research. 3

(b) Outline stages of product development. 4

(c) Explain the benefits of branding to an organisation. 3

4. (a) Describe the methods used by an organisation to ensure a quality product. 4

(b) Outline the factors that may be considered when choosing a suitable method of production. 3

(c) Explain the impact of over-stocking on the organisation. 3

5. (a) Identify **2** pieces of legislation that exist to protect employees. 2

(b) (i) Identify **2** methods of selecting the right person for a job. 2

   (ii) Explain **one** benefit of each method identified in 5(b)(i). 2

(c) Outline the effect of industrial action. 4

6. (a) Discuss advantages and disadvantages of being a private limited company. 4

(b) Describe the influence of stakeholders on a private limited company. 4

(c) Identify **2** internal factors that could affect the success of an organisation. 2

[Turn over

MARKS

7. (a) An organisation has provided the following financial information.

     Using the table below, calculate the missing information for (i), (ii) and (iii).   3

Units	Fixed Costs £	Variable Costs £	Total Costs £
0	1,000	0	1,000
100	(i)	2,000	3,000
200	1,000	4,000	(ii)
300	1,000	(iii)	7,000

   (b) Describe the use of technology in the finance department.   4

   (c) Define the following financial terms from an Income Statement: 3
   *   Expenses
   *   Profit for the Year
   *   Gross Profit.

[END OF QUESTION PAPER]

[BLANK PAGE]

DO NOT WRITE ON THIS PAGE

NATIONAL 5

Answers

SQA NATIONAL 5
BUSINESS MANAGEMENT 2018

Questions that ask candidates to **Describe** . . .
Candidates must make a number of relevant, factual points up to the total mark allocation for the question. These should be key points. The points do not need to be in any particular order. Candidates may provide a number of straightforward points or a smaller number of developed points, or a combination of these.

Up to the total mark allocation for this question:
• 1 mark should be given for each accurate relevant point of knowledge.
• a second mark could be given for any point that is developed from the point of knowledge.

Questions that ask candidates to **Explain** . . .
Candidates must make a number of points that relate cause and effect and/or make the relationships between things clear, for example by showing connections between a process/situation. These should be key reasons and may include theoretical concepts. There is no need to prioritise the reasons.

Candidates may provide a number of straightforward reasons or a smaller number of developed reasons, or a combination of these.

Up to the total mark allocation for this question:
• 1 mark should be given for each accurate relevant point of reason.
• a second mark could be given for any other point that is developed from the same reason.

Section 1

1. (a) (i) Sole trader

    (ii) Responses could include:
    • From the case study — Gemma likes to offer a personal and tailored service to her customers to meet their needs
    • Providing extra assistance to a customer to ensure that their needs are completely satisfied

    (b) Responses could include:
    Costs
    • Web hosting
    • Website development and maintenance
    • Postage charges for sending out goods to customers

    Benefits
    • Increased market share
    • Ability to operate nationally/internationally
    • "Free" advertising

    (c) Responses could include:
    • Advertising, e.g. radio, newspaper
    • Customer demonstrations
    • Free offers
    • Competitions
    • Discounts

    (d) Responses could include:
    • Staff get better at their job
    • Increased motivation
    • It is easier to introduce changes
    • The image of the organisation is improved
    • Staff become more flexible

    (e) Responses could include:
    • Rent
    • Electricity
    • Business rates
    • Advertising

2. (a) (i) Responses could include:
    • It reuses unwanted materials
    • It reduces the amount of waste going to landfill
    • Employ refugees
    • Not using 'sweatshop' conditions

    (ii) Responses could include:
    • Limits the amount of waste going to landfill
    • Improves the image of the organisation
    • Increases sales/profits
    • Can be used as a USP
      ◦ Can give a competitive edge
      ◦ Can win awards
    • Can reduce costs if waste materials are used

    (b) Responses could include:
    • Access to more customers thus chances of increased market share/profit
    • Access to customer information thereby allowing it to target products/marketing to those most likely to buy
    • Can gain customer feedback thereby can change things to gain better customer satisfaction
    • Customers can shop 24/7 which gives the organisation maximum time for customers to buy
    • Can show entire product line thereby increasing customer choice
    • Reduces costs as fixtures and fittings for shops are not required

    (c) (i) Responses could include:
    • On the job
    • Induction training

    (ii) Responses could include:
    On the job
    • Employees become familiar with surroundings
    • May be cheaper than other forms of training
    • Employees are actually productive
    • Tailored to company needs

    Induction
    • Employees will feel at ease
    • Employees will become familiar with the people and the surroundings
    • Employees will become aware of health and safety issues

    (d) Responses could include:
    Application Form/CV
    • These contain personal information on a candidate
    • They can be used to compare against the person specification

    Interview
    • Allows the organisation to ask a series of questions
      ◦ To allow for comparisons
    • Allows the organisation to assess the candidate's appearance/personality
    • Allows them to question the content of the CV/application form
    • Allows a candidate to ask questions

Reference
- Provides key information on attendance, attitude, time-keeping
- Usually written by a past employer
- Allows an organisation to confirm the content of a CV/application form

Testing
- These provide additional information on a candidate's suitability through practical assessment
- An organisation can see how a candidate copes under pressure

(e) Responses could include:
Quality Circles
- Small groups of employees who meet regularly to discuss how to improve methods of working

Quality Assurance
- Checking at every stage of the production process
  - To ensure 'right first time' and prevent errors

Quality Control
- Checking at the beginning and the end of production process only

Quality Standards
- When the product reaches the required standard it can be awarded a quality logo
  - Gives consumers confidence

Quality Inputs
- Raw materials need to be quality in order to obtain a quality final product
- All staff must be trained so they are competent and are all working to the same quality standards
- Machines need to be maintained so that they do not make mistakes affecting quality

Benchmarking
- Trying to match the standard of the quality leader/competitor

Section 2

3. (a) (i) Responses could include:
  - Staff/HR
  - Management/HR
  - Finance
  - Technology

(ii) Responses could include:
Staff
- If staff are trained they will be more productive
- If staff are more motivated they may produce a higher quality service
- If staff feel they have a say in decision making they may be more loyal to the organisation

Finance
- If there is a surplus of cash then the organisation may be able to make improvements
- If there is a lack of finance cost cutting measures need to be considered

Management
- If their objectives differ from the organisation's then the overall strategic aims of the business may not be met
- The quality of their decisions e.g. the range of goods they decide to stock can mean that the organisation improves customer satisfaction

Technology
- Having up-to-date technology will allow the organisation to produce quality products
- Having up-to-date technology may give the firm a competitive edge

(b) Responses could include:
- Provide a service to others
- Raise awareness of issues
- Better service for the community
- Creating a better reputation
- Ensuring finances are kept within budget
- Be socially responsible

(c) Responses could include:
Advantages
- The owner is hands-on to provide a personal service
- Owners get to keep all their profits
- Easy to set up
  - Fewer legal restrictions
- Can make all the decisions
  - This is faster as no arguments

Disadvantages
- Limited access to finance
- No-one to consult or share ideas with
- Difficult to take time off for holidays or if off sick
- Liability is unlimited
  - The owners may lose their personal possessions in order to meet the debts of the organisation

4. (a) (i) Responses could include:
Word processing package
- Create a job advert/application form
- Key in a job or person specification
- Letter to applicants about interview/successful appointments/unsuccessful notification

(ii) **Database package**
- Record of applicants
- Record of posts available

(iii) **Company website**
- Online application form
- Electronic job and person specifications could be accessed online
- Contact us feature to apply for jobs
- Internal jobs could be posted on the website

(b) (i) Responses could include:
- Sit in
- Overtime ban
- Work to rule
- Go slow
- Strike
- Boycott
- Lock out
- Protest/picket line

(ii) Responses could include:
- Production within the organisation may come to a halt therefore the organisation could struggle to produce goods to meet customer demand
  - Causing customers to go elsewhere
- Decreased levels of production could damage the reputation of the organisation
- An organisation could lose customers as goods not produced within an acceptable timescale
- Employees refusing to work overtime or going slow would mean deadlines not met
  - Creating a poor image or reputation
- Company's share price may fall due to the poor reputation of the firm

(c) Responses could include:
- Software packages with remote access allow flexible working arrangements
- Video conferencing allows employees in different locations to take part in the same meetings
  - Less travel time and fewer costs are incurred
- Email allows an employee to communicate with their job share partner/communicate with the office from home
  - Easier access to others with the use of email
- Allows work to be completed outside of 'traditional' working hours
- Less office space required as staff may be working from home using laptops
- Electronic documents can be shared and stored on the cloud/intranet to be used out with the office

5. (a) (i) Responses could include:
- Increasing wages
- Increasing purchases
- £20,000 spent on capital expenditure
- Negative closing balance in May and June

(ii) Responses could include:
- Do not allow overtime
- Reduce the number of workers to reduce wages
- Find a cheaper supplier to reduce cost of purchases
  - Negotiate discounts for bulk buying or prompt payment
- Purchasing the van on hire purchase
  - To spread payments
- Lease or rent the van rather than buying it outright
- Arrange for an overdraft to cover negative closing balance.
- Take out a bank loan to boost receipts

(b) (i) Responses could include:
- Advertising

(ii) Responses could include:
- Purchases
- Wages

(c) Responses could include:
- To calculate gross profit
- To calculate the cost of sales
- To show net sales
- To calculate the total cost of expenses
- To calculate profit for the year/net profit
- To show other incomes
- For legal reasons
- To aid decision making
- For tax reasons

6. (a) Responses could include:
Job
- Where a one off/unique product is made
- Each job is started and finished before moving on to the next

Batch
- When groups of similar products are produced
- Machinery is stopped, cleaned etc. before being used for a different batch

Flow
- A continuous process is used and goods move along a production line from beginning to end
- Large volumes can be made in a short period of time
- Each product is identical

(b) Responses could include:
- Price reflects the quality given
- Quality of the raw materials is consistent
- Delivery time meets the needs of the organisation
- The supplier can deliver the correct quantity
- The level of credit being offered by the supplier
- The length of credit period being offered by the supplier
- Location of supplier as it will impact on delivery charges/time

(c) Responses could include:
Under stocking
- Becomes harder to cope with unexpected changes in demand which means customers may go elsewhere to purchase the product
  - If customers go elsewhere they may lose them completely and not just the one time
- Production may have to stop completely meaning paying for workers who aren't producing any goods
- Continually ordering or restocking can mean increased administration costs
  - Increased transport costs
- Increased unit costs due to not bulk buying

Over stocking
- Carry large amounts of stock will increase the cost of storage which reduces profit
  - May result in having to pay larger insurance costs
  - Increased security costs
- Capital is tied up in stock which means that the money cannot be used elsewhere
- The stock may deteriorate resulting in larger wastage costs
- Changes in trends and fashion will mean that stock might become obsolete and not be able to be sold
- Higher risk of theft as it is less obvious when stock has gone missing

NATIONAL 5 BUSINESS MANAGEMENT 2017

Questions that ask candidates to **Describe** …
Candidates must make a number of relevant, factual points up to the total mark allocation for the question. These should be key points. The points do not need to be in any particular order. Candidates may provide a number of straightforward points or a smaller number of developed points, or a combination of these.

Up to the total mark allocation for this question:
- 1 mark should be given for each accurate relevant point of knowledge
- a second mark could be given for any point that is developed from the point of knowledge

Questions that ask candidates to **Explain** …
Candidates must make a number of points that relate cause and effect and/or make the relationships between things clear, for example by showing connections between a process/situation. These should be key reasons and may include theoretical concepts. There is no need to prioritise the reasons.

Candidates may provide a number of straightforward reasons or a smaller number of developed reasons, or a combination of these.

Up to the total mark allocation for this question:
- 1 mark should be given for each accurate relevant point of reason

- a second mark could be given for any other point that is developed from the same reason

Questions that ask candidates to **Compare** …
Candidates must demonstrate a true comparison (like with like) in order to gain any mark. Both sides of the point must be clear but need not be linked (can be matched up). Candidates can write several points regarding the first comparison item followed by several points on the second and the marker match the points using codes (e.g. a, b, c).

Up to the total mark allocation for this question:
- 1 mark should be given for each compared point

Section 1

1. (a) (i) Responses should include:
   - Restaurant reviews in newspapers
   - Branding
   - Shop/Shop Premises
   - Website
   - Social Media (accept names – e.g. Facebook, Twitter, etc.)

   (ii) Responses could include:
   - Brand advertises/promotes the product which increases brand recognition
     - Reduces spending on promotion/increases sales/increases profits
   - Customer loyalty which will lead to repeat purchases
   - Perception of quality which means customers will choose over rivals
   - Ability to charge higher prices which leads to increased revenues/profits

   (b) (i) Responses could include:
   - Road
   - Sea
   - Rail
   - Air

   (ii) Responses could include:
   Road
   - Direct distribution
   - Cheaper than rail/air transport
   - Difficult to carry large amounts
   - Slower method of distribution compared with sea/rail/air
   - Not environmentally friendly
     - Increases pollution

   Sea
   - Cheaper than rail/air transport
   - Large items can be transported
   - Slower method of transport than road/rail/air
   - Requires additional transport/not direct

   Rail
   - Large items can be transported
   - Quicker than road/sea
   - Reduces carbon footprint
   - Requires additional transport/not direct

   Air
   - Fast method of distribution
   - Expensive method

   (c) Responses could include:
   Political
   - Health and safety standards affect the business as they will have to train staff to follow guidelines
     - Will increase costs to provide these
   - Health and safety standards affect the business as they will have to provide safety equipment/clothing
   - EU legislation protects the brand name
     - Reduces impact of competitors

   Competition
   - Rivals could try to steal customers from the business
     - Which would reduce sales/profits/market share

   Technology
   - Social media increases customer awareness

   Social
   - Change in taste can lead to increased/higher demand

   (d) Responses could include:
   - A sole trader is owned by one person whereas a private limited company is owned by shareholders
   - A sole trader is run by an individual whereas a private limited company is run by a managing director/board of directors
   - A sole trader makes the decisions in a business whereas a managing director/board of directors/shareholders make decisions in a private limited company
   - Sole traders have unlimited liability whereas private limited companies have limited liability
   - Both belong to the private sector of the economy
   - Legal documents required on forming a private limited company whereas a sole trader does not require any formal paperwork

2. (a) (i) Responses should include:
   - Lifestyle
   - Health conscious
   - Beauty conscious
   - Chocolate lovers
   - Ethical buyers
   - Organic buyers

   (ii) Responses could include:
   - Able to adapt product to suit target market
   - Pricing strategy will be appropriate to target market
   - Appropriate places to sell product will be chosen
   - Reduces likelihood of wasted investment in wrong product/promotions
   - Can offer a range of products to suit different markets

   (b) (i) Responses could include:
   - Batch production – where a group of identical products are made with all processes being carried out simultaneously
   - Flow production – where products are made in stages on a production line with processes being added at each stage

   (ii) Responses could include:
   Batch
   Advantages
   - Large amounts can be made
   - Batches can be customised
     - Meeting customer needs
   - Economies of scale gained

   Disadvantages
   - Expensive initial outlay for equipment
   - Careful production planning required

- Equipment needs to be cleaned between batches
- Mistakes may lead to loss of whole batch
  - This can lead to a loss of profits

Flow

Advantages
- High quantity of products
- Standardisation of quality of products
- Economies of scale gained
  - Lower cost per unit of production
- Machines can work 24/7

Disadvantages
- Expensive initial outlay for equipment
- Maintenance costs
- Lack of output if machines are broken

(c) Responses could include:
- More expensive to purchase environmentally friendly/hybrid vehicles, e.g. LPG fuel/electric
- Reduces environmental damage/pollution
- Costs of using ethical suppliers may be higher
- Helps business to meet government targets
- Efficiency may fall, ethical distribution may reduce amount of deliveries
- Gives a competitive edge over rivals
- Creates a positive image for the business/good CSR
  - Customer loyalty could increase

(d) Responses should include:
Owners
- Make decisions that could affect product development
- Invest more money which can aid expansion

Suppliers
- Can increase price which increases production cost
  - This reduces profit margins

Customers/Independent Retailers/Health Centres
- Customer satisfaction will impact upon sales and revenues
- Customer loyalty which means repeat purchases
- Customer recommendations which leads to increased sales

Section 2

3. (a) (i) Responses could include:
- Private
- Public
- Third/voluntary

(ii) Responses could include:
- Both the third and public sector organisations have the objective to make a difference
- Private sector organisations have an objective to make a profit whereas a public sector organisation has the objective to use public funds effectively
- Third sector organisations have an objective to increase awareness/sales whereas public sector organisation has the objective to provide a service
- All sectors have the objective to be socially responsible

(b) Responses could include:
- Have a good aftersales service
- Have a returns policy
- Ensure all staff are highly trained
- Keep staff motivated
- Use quality indicators to measure performance
- Recruit suitable staff, e.g. helpful, polite, etc.
- Use high quality raw materials/quality control
- Ensure system of customer feedback is in place

(c) Responses could include:
- A lack of finance means not having enough money to carry out expansion plans
- Having excess finances that enables an organisation to train staff, invest in more equipment etc.
- If staff are skilled they will provide good quality customer service
- The morale of staff to carry out their jobs to a high standard
- Available technology used within the organisation could increase the rate of production
- If technology breaks down this can result in delays in production
- If managers are inexperienced they could make poor decisions

4. (a) Responses could include:
Job description
- States the tasks and responsibilities of the job
  - Includes the conditions of the post, e.g. pay, hours

Person specification
- Describes the ideal candidate for the post
  - Contains the essential and desirable characteristics
  - Skills, qualities and qualifications necessary to do the job

Job advert
- Usually contains aspects of the job description and person specification
  - Could be placed internally or externally
  - Internally on the organisation's intranet, noticeboards etc.
  - Externally in newspapers, job centres etc.

Application form
- Standard form sent out by an organisation for candidates to complete using personal details

(b) Responses could include:
- Internal recruitment ensures candidates already have knowledge of the organisation, however external recruitment can attract candidates with new ideas
- Internal recruitment is fast as candidates are already in the organisation, however external recruitment can take a very long time
- Internal recruitment is more cost effective as advertising can be done on staff newsletters or intranet, whereas external recruitment can be very expensive in costs of advertising
- Internal recruitment can create another vacancy, whereas external recruitment adds a new employee to the staff
- Internal recruitment is motivating for staff who see a promotion path, however external recruitment may cause conflict with existing staff
- Internal vacancies can be advertised on noticeboards and via email, whereas external vacancies can be advertised using websites and job centres

(c) Responses could include:
- Employees who are trained will have better skills meaning a higher quality output
- Employees who are trained will be more efficient at their job which means productivity will increase
- Employees will be more motivated which means they are less likely to be absent
- Employees may gain qualifications which may give them more incentive to remain with the organisations
- Employees may be able to gain experience which can help them to achieve promotion

(d) Responses could include:
- Protection against discrimination
- Protected characteristics
- Age/sex/sexual orientation/gender re-assignment/ disability/race, religion or belief/marriage or civil partnership/pregnancy and maternity
- Includes workplace victimisation, harassment and bullying

5. (a) Responses could include:
Internet
- Ordering inventory online

Database/EPOS
- The use of bar codes can be used to keep a running total of inventory in hand
- It can be useful for the re-ordering of inventory as can be linked directly to supplier
- It can help staff to locate inventory within the warehouse

CAM (Computer Aided Manufacture)
- Could be used to help control the machinery of the business
- This would allow for capital intensive production to run smoothly

CAD (Computer Aided Design)
- Could be used to help design products on a computer screen
- This would allow for problems to be solved before prototypes are made

GPS
- Could allow an organisation to keep track of deliveries

(b) (i) Responses could include:
Quality control
- Quality is checked at the beginning (inputs) and end (outputs) of the production process only
- Unacceptable products are either scrapped or put back for reworking

Quality assurance
- Quality is checked at every stage of the production process
- Mistakes are found early in the process
  - Less waste

Quality inputs
- Ensuring that raw materials are the best that they can be to ensure a quality output
- Ensuring that machinery and equipment is up-to-date and fully serviced so that it is working to its best at all times
- Ensuring the recruitment process gets the best staff
- Training staff to ensure they can produce goods to the best quality

(ii) Responses could include:
Maximum inventory (stock) level
- The highest level of inventory that should be held at any one time

Lead time
- The time from placing the order to the goods being delivered

6. (a) Responses should include:
- A — Sales revenue/Sales/Revenue
- B — 30,000
- C — 20,000

(b) (i) Responses could include:
- Retained profits — reinvested from previous years
- Share issue — selling shares to friends and family (Ltd)
- Bank loan — money borrowed from the bank repaid with interest/OR in instalments
- Government grant — money received from the government that does not need to be repaid
- Overdraft — taking more money out of your bank account than is present in your account
- Mortgage — money borrowed to buy property
- Hire purchase — purchasing assets and repaying over time with interest
- Leasing — renting equipment/assets

(ii) Responses could include:
Retained profits
- Cash is readily available
- Does not have to be paid back
- No interest charged

Share issue
- No interest charged
- Does not have to be repaid

Bank loan
- Repaid in instalments
  - Aids budgeting

Government grant
- Does not need to be paid back

Overdraft
- Easy to arrange
- Only pay interest on amount borrowed

Mortgage
- Repaid over a long period of time
- Large amount can be raised

Hire purchase
- Costs spread over a period of time
- Helps cash flow issues

Leasing
- Can acquire an expensive asset without a capital outlay
- Easier to change equipment when it becomes obsolete

(c) Responses could include:
- To make comparisons between actual and projected figures
- Take corrective action
- To allow the organisation to make better decisions
- Identify surplus of cash/identify a deficit
- To set targets
- Budgets can be used to plan for the future

NATIONAL 5 BUSINESS MANAGEMENT 2017 SPECIMEN QUESTION PAPER

Questions that ask candidates to **Describe** . . .
Candidates must make a number of relevant, factual points up to the total mark allocation for the question. These should be key points. The points do not need to be in any particular order. Candidates may provide a number of straightforward points or a smaller number of developed points, or a combination of these.

Up to the total mark allocation for this question:
- 1 mark should be given for each accurate relevant point of knowledge

- a second mark could be given for any point that is developed from the point of knowledge.

Questions that ask candidates to **Explain** . . .
Candidates must make a number of points that relate cause and effect and/or make the relationships between things clear, for example by showing connections between a process/situation. These should be key reasons and may include theoretical concepts. There is no need to prioritise the reasons. Candidates may provide a number of straightforward reasons or a smaller number of developed reasons, or a combination of these.

Up to the total mark allocation for this question:
- 1 mark should be given for each accurate relevant point of reason
- a second mark could be given for any other point that is developed from the same reason.

Questions that ask candidates to **Compare** . . .
Candidates must demonstrate a true comparison in order to gain any mark. Both sides of the point must be clear but need not be linked. Candidates can write several points regarding the first comparison item, followed by several points on the second, and the marker match the points using codes (e.g. a, b, c).

Section 1

Up to the total mark allocation for this question:
- 1 mark should be given for each compared point

1. (a) (i) Responses could include:
   - They do not add any artificial colourings etc.
   - They recycle their waste by turning it into feed for pigs
   - Using labour rather than machines (hand pressed)

   (ii) Responses could include:
   - Limits the amount of waste going to landfill
   - Helps to win awards
   - Reduce costs/increase costs
   - Can charge a higher price
   - Improves the image of the organisation
     ○ This could increase sales/profits
   - Can be used as a USP
     ○ Can give a competitive edge

   (b) Responses could include:
   - Job Production
     ○ More labour intensive
     ○ One product is made at a time
     ○ Uses skilled labour
     ○ Production costs are higher
     ○ Can customise individual products
     ○ More motivating as the product changes

   Whereas
   - Flow Production
     ○ More capital intensive
     ○ Multiple products are made at a time
     ○ Uses unskilled labour
     ○ Can spread cost over multiple units/can benefit from economies of scale
     ○ Creates standardised products
     ○ Less motivating as task is repetitive
   - Both methods of production can be expensive in terms of staff training and machinery

   (c) (i) Responses could include:
   - More profitable to produce than cider
   - 67% of customers rated "all natural" as the most interesting products
   - 60% globally say they are interested in products with proven health benefits

   (ii) Responses could include:
   Political
   - Changes in laws may prevent Cuddybridge from operating, which will result in it having to spend extra finance to comply with the changes
   - Local council may refuse to give planning permission, which means that the company cannot grow

   Economic
   - There may be a reduction in consumer spending due to recession, which will reduce sales
   - Cost of producing the apple juice may rise due to inflation, which will increase variable costs

   Social
   - There may be an increase in publicity about healthy drinks, which may increase sales

   Technological
   - A new piece of equipment may become available, which would increase the speed of the pressing

   Environmental
   - Weather may be bad, which could result in a shortage of apples
     ○ This could halt production
   - There may be increased consumer awareness of environmental issues, which may mean Cuddybridge may have to adapt packaging

   (d) Responses could include:
   Quality Circles
   - Small groups of employees who meet regularly to discuss how to improve methods of working

   Quality Assurance
   - Checking at every stage of the production process
   - To ensure 'right first time' and prevent errors

   Quality Control
   - Checking at (the beginning and) the end of production process only

   Quality Inputs
   - Raw materials need to be high quality in order to obtain a quality final product
   - All staff must be trained so they are competent and are all working to the same quality standards
   - Machines need to be maintained so that they do not make mistakes affecting quality

   (e) (i) Road
   (ii) Responses could include:
   - Juice is delivered directly to the customer (door to door)
   - Juice can be transported in refrigerated vans
   - Cuddybridge can deliver at any time of the day or night
   - Clients are local so air (or sea) is not suitable

2. (a) (i) Responses could include:
   - On the Job
   - Off the Job

   (ii) Responses could include:
   On the Job
   Advantages
   - Employees become familiar with surroundings
   - May be cheaper than other forms of training
     ○ As existing staff can train others
   - Employees are productive during training
   - Training is specific to the organisation
   - Takes place in work time so employees may be happier to take part

Disadvantages
- Takes a current employee away from production
  - Reduces the amount produced
- Employees may make mistakes whilst learning
  - Results in increased wastage/lower customer satisfaction

Off the Job
Advantages
- Employees may gain a qualification
  - This could result in them being considered for promotion
- Wider range of skills can be gained
  - Improves staff flexibility
- Can learn from outside experts

Disadvantages
- No production takes place
- Expensive as have to pay for the course/outside training providers
  - Also pay for staff travel expenses
- May need to hire a supply/temporary worker

(b) Responses could include:
Application Form/CV
- A document which contains personal information on a candidate
  - They can be used to compare against the person specification
  - Can be used to decide who is short-listed for interview/who is rejected

Interview
- A face to face meeting where an applicant is asked questions
  - Allows the organisation to ask a series of questions to all applicants to allow for comparisons
  - Allows the organisation to assess the candidate's appearance/personality
  - Allows the organisation to question the content of the CV/application form
  - Allows a candidate to ask questions

Reference
- A written or oral report on the work ethic of an applicant provided by a previous employer
  - Provides key information on attendance, attitude, time-keeping
  - Usually written by a past employer
  - Allows an organisation to confirm the content of a CV/application form

Testing
- A physical or mental challenge for the applicant
  - These provide additional information on a candidate's suitability
  - An organisation can see how a candidate copes under pressure

(c) Responses could include:
- Fifteen aims to help young people whereas a private sector organisation aims to grow
- Both Fifteen and a private sector organisation aim to make a profit
- Both Fifteen and a private sector organisation aim to provide a service

(d) Responses could include:
- Consumers are attracted to the product, in an attempt to be like the celebrity
- Jamie Oliver is already a household name, so Fifteen could save money on marketing

- Higher prices can be charged, which will result in greater profits
- Greater chance of success, as Jamie Oliver will already have brand loyalty

(e) Responses could include:
Marketing
- Internet could be used to allow customers to book tables online
- Internet could be used to gather customer information through online surveys
- MS Publisher could be used to create business cards/posters
- Apps could be created to inform customers
  - Send push notifications to increase awareness of products
  - Allow customers to purchase goods on the go
- Social media could be used to increase awareness of products/notify customers of special offers
  - These can be shared or re-tweeted to increase brand awareness
- QR codes could be used to create a link to Fifteen's website

Operations
- Ovens could be programmed to come on and go off at certain times of the day
- iPads could be used to take orders from customers
  - These would automatically send orders to the kitchen
- Databases could be used to create/maintain stock records/customer records
- Internet could be used to compare the prices of suppliers

(f) Responses could include:
- Find a cheaper supplier of ingredients
- Negotiate a cheaper rental agreement on restaurants
- Switch utility suppliers
- Reduce the amount of expenditure on advertising

Section 2

3. (a) (i) Responses could include:
- Employees
- Shareholders/owners
- Government
- Suppliers
- Bank
- Local Community
- Customers

(ii) Responses could include:
- Employees
  - Could go on strike, preventing production
  - Could provide poor customer service, which will reduce sales
- Shareholders/owners
  - Could invest additional capital, allowing more efficient equipment to be purchased
    - This could reduce wastage
- Government
  - Could increase National Living Wage, which will increase wages
  - Could change taxation levels, resulting in lower profits
- Suppliers
  - Could deliver goods late, which would prevent production
    - This would result in disappointed customers

- ◦ May increase prices, which will result in reduction of gross profit
  - Bank
    - ◦ Could refuse an overdraft, making it more difficult to pay bills
  - Local Community
    - ◦ Could protest about the business, leading to a bad reputation

(b) Responses could include:
- Train staff
  - ◦ So they are knowledgeable and can answer customer queries
- Maintain a clean environment
- Employ extra staff to cover busy periods
  - ◦ This will reduce queues
- Use effective pricing strategies
- Provide a quick response to complaints
- Provide a good aftersales service

(c) Responses could include:
- Sole Trader is owned by one person whereas an LTD owned by shareholders
- Sole Trader has unlimited liability whereas an LTD has limited liability
- Does not require any formal paperwork to begin trading whereas an LTD must prepare formal documents to be sent to Register House
- Sole Trader keeps all profits whereas an LTD splits profits (dividends) with the shareholders

4. (a) (i) Responses could include:
- The price the customers are willing to pay for it
- The price competitors are charging
- The stage of the product life cycle
- The image of the product
- The cost of the raw materials
- Location of retail outlet

(ii) Responses could include:
- Premium/High Price, where the price is set higher than competitor
- Market price, where prices are set at a similar level to competitors
- Low price, where prices are set lower than competitors

(b) Responses could include:
- Brand loyalty, which means you are guaranteed returning customers
- Brand recognition, so less advertising required
- Gives an illusion/image of quality, which means higher prices can be charged
- Easier to launch new products, due to customers being familiar with the brand

(c) Responses could include:
- Use technology to reduce the amount of paper used
- Ensure that adverts comply with discrimination laws, e.g. do not exploit women in adverts
- Ensure that adverts do not give misleading information
- Ensure that adverts do not offend customers' beliefs
- Ensure that there are no hidden costs in adverts

5. (a) Responses could include:
- Identify the vacancy
- Carry out a job analysis
- Create a job description
- Create a person specification
- Advertise the job
- Send out application forms

(b) Responses could include:
- Piece rate — employee is paid for each item they produce
- Time rate — employee paid for each hour they work
- Overtime — employee paid for working more than their contracted hours
  - ◦ This could be paid at a higher rate, e.g. time and a half, double time
- Bonus — an additional payment over and above normal salary
- Commission — employee is paid a percentage of their overall sales
- Salary — an annual amount paid in 12 equal instalments

(c) Responses could include:
- Equality Act
- Health and Safety at Work Act
- National Minimum Wage/National Living Wage Regulations
- Employment Rights Act

6. (a) (i) £20,000
       (ii) £8,000

(b) Responses could include:
Bank loan
- Finance borrowed from a bank and repaid with interest
  - ◦ Paid back in instalments
  - ◦ Paid over a long period of time
  - ◦ Interest is payable on amount borrowed

Grant
- Cash given to a business by the government
  - ◦ Cash does not need to be repaid
  - ◦ Complex paperwork will need to be completed
  - ◦ Set criteria may need to be met

Overdraft
- Can take more cash out than you have in your account
  - ◦ Suitable for short-term cash flow problems
  - ◦ Cash available quickly as it can be prearranged

Share Issue
- People are invited to buy a part ownership of a business
  - ◦ Investment does not need to be repaid
  - ◦ Large amounts can be raised
  - ◦ Control is not lost to outsiders
  - ◦ Dividends will need to be paid

(c) Responses could include:
- Formulae can be used to calculate information
  - ◦ Which allows for automatic calculation if anything changes
  - ◦ Which reduces error
- Information can be saved and edited later
- Templates can be used for financial information, e.g. Cash Budgets/Profit Statements
- Standardisation of documents means that processes are easily replicated
- Graphs/Charts can be created to display information
  - ◦ Which allows easier comparison of complex financial information

(d) Responses could include:
- To calculate gross profit
- To calculate the cost of sales
- To show net sales
- To calculate the total cost of expenses
- To calculate profit for the year/net profit
- To show other incomes

- For legal reasons
- To aid decision making
- For tax reasons

7. (a) Responses could include:
- Is the price reasonable?
- Is the quality acceptable?
- Quality of the raw materials is consistent
- Delivery time meets the needs of the organisation
- The supplier can deliver the correct quantity
- The length of credit period being offered by the supplier
- Location of supplier as it will impact on delivery charges/time
- Discounts that could be given for bulk buying
- Is the supplier reliable/do they deliver on time?

(b)
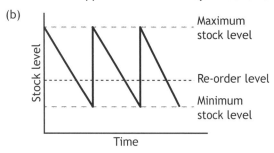

(c) Responses could include:
Overstocking
- Carrying large amounts of stock will increase the cost of storage, which reduces profit
  - May result in having to pay larger insurance costs
  - Increased security costs
- Capital is tied up in stock, which means that the finance cannot be used elsewhere
- The stock may deteriorate, resulting in larger wastage costs
- Changes in trends and fashion will mean that stock might become obsolete, which means it will not be able to be sold
- Higher risk of theft, as it is less obvious that stock has gone missing

Understocking
- Becomes harder to cope with unexpected changes in demand, which means customers may go elsewhere to purchase the product
  - If customers go elsewhere the firm may lose them completely and not just the one time
- Production may have to stop completely, meaning paying for workers who are not producing any goods
- Need to continually order or restock, which can mean increased administration costs
  - Increased transport costs
- No bulk buying, therefore increased unit costs

Questions that ask candidates to **Describe** . . .
Candidates must make a number of relevant, factual points up to the total mark allocation for the question. These should be key points/features. The points do not need to be in any particular order. Candidates may provide a number of straightforward points or a smaller number of developed points, or a combination of these.

Up to the total mark allocation for this question:
- 1 mark should be given for each accurate relevant point of knowledge
- a second mark could be given for any point that is developed from the point of knowledge.

Questions that ask candidates to **Explain** . . .
Candidates must make a number of points that relate cause and effect and/or make the relationships between things clear, for example by showing connections between a process/situation. These should be key reasons and may include theoretical concepts. There is no need to prioritise the reasons.

Candidates may provide a number of straightforward reasons or a smaller number of developed reasons, or a combination of these.

Up to the total mark allocation for this question:
- 1 mark should be given for each accurate relevant point of reason
- a second mark could be given for any other point that is developed from the same reason

Questions that ask candidates to **Compare** . . .
Candidates must demonstrate a true comparison in order to gain any mark. Both sides of the point must be clear but need not be linked. Candidates can write several points regarding the first comparison item, followed by several points on the second, and the marker match the points using codes (e.g. a, b, c)

Up to the total mark allocation for this question:
- 1 mark should be given for each compared point

Section 1

1. (a) (i) *Outline 2 steps, from the case study, for a maximum of 2 marks.*
Responses could include:
- Pre-measuring ingredients/reducing food waste.
- Limiting its packaging.
- Sourcing food from local British suppliers/ minimising its carbon footprint.
- All boxes, brown bags and spice containers are recyclable.
- Using compostable wool liners.

(ii) *1 mark for each valid explanation, to a maximum of 3 marks.*
Responses could include:
- Some customers are more environmentally aware — therefore more likely to buy.
- Uses local suppliers — which reduces carbon footprint.
- May reduce customer/local community complaints — therefore improving the image of the business.
  - Encourage loyalty.

- Good for advertising/PR — which improves its image.
  - May be a USP.
- Awareness of recycling is increasing — so customers want to purchase from businesses that use reduced/recyclable packaging.
  - This could increase sales revenue.
- Can be cheaper to produce/reduce costs to the business — as recycled materials could be used.
- Will meet local council targets — meaning less chance of receiving a fine.

(b) (i) *1 mark for a valid identification of the trend.*
Responses could include:
- Increased/grown/increased demand.
- Number of meals delivered grown to 800,000 in 2015.

(ii) *Describe 2 factors to gain full marks. 1 mark for each valid description.*
Responses could include:
Political
- Government encouraging healthy eating.
- Introduction of 'sugar tax'.

Economic
- Improving state of the economy.
- Increased disposable income.

Social factors
- Changing tastes and fashions e.g. healthy eating.
- People have different work patterns leading to higher demand for convenience foods.
- Increased number of cooking programmes on television.

Technology
- Creation of website and apps allows for easy ordering.
- Social media has raised awareness of the industry.

Environmental
- Customers encouraged to reduce their wastage and/or improving their carbon footprint.
- Customers are more environmentally aware.

Competitive
- Increasing price of eating out.

(c) *Describe at least 2 factors that influence the choice of supplier to a maximum of four marks. 1 mark for each valid description of the factor, up to 3 marks for any one factor.*
Responses could include:
- The cost of the raw materials.
  - Costs need to be kept to a minimum to maximise profit.
- The quality of the raw materials.
- The quantity of raw materials required.
- The time taken from ordering to delivery of raw materials (lead time).
- How reliable/dependable the supplier is.
  - If goods are delivered late production may be held up.
- The location of the supplier.
  - If supplier is far away then deliveries may take longer.
- Cost of delivery of the raw materials.
- Discounts available.
  - This will reduce costs.
- Availability of trade credit.

(d) *Describe at least 2 methods to a maximum of 3 marks. 1 mark for each valid description, up to 2 marks for any one method. Maximum 2 marks for advertising.*
Responses could include:
- BOGOF: buy one get one free.
- Give customers a free item (gift) when they join.
- Free samples to try the item before you buy.
- Loyalty card: customers are awarded a set number of points depending on how much they spend.
- Free entry to competitions when you buy the product to win a prize.
- Demonstrations of products where customers see/try new product before buying.
- Free delivery — goods delivered free of charge with purchase.
- TV advertising: producing audio-visual images to give information during commercial breaks.
- Radio advertising: producing a radio advert sometimes with catchy tunes that can be played on local or national radio stations.
- Newspaper/magazine advertising: images and information can be printed in local or national papers.
- Outdoor media/billboards/transport: large images can be shown to the public.
- Social media using networking sites to share information.

(e) *Describe at least 2 sources of finance to a maximum of 5 marks. 1 mark for each valid description of source, up to 4 marks for any one source.*
Responses could include:
Bank loan
- Money borrowed from the bank which is repaid with interest <u>or</u> instalments.
  - Paid back in instalments/with interest.

Grant
- Money received from the government which does not need to be repaid <u>or</u> conditions attached.
  - Conditions may need to be met/is not repaid.
  - Takes a long time due to paperwork.

Overdraft
- Can take more money out than you have in your account.

Retained profits
- Profits made by the business in previous years which is reused.
- No interest is payable.
- Will reduce the amount available for dividends.

Share issue
- Inviting people to buy a share in the business.
  - Shareholders will have a say in decision making.

Mortgage
- Money borrowed from the bank to purchase property.
- Interest is charged.
- Long term to repay.
- Repaid in instalments.

2. (a) (i) *1 mark for correctly identifying the sector.*
- Third sector/voluntary sector.

(ii) *1 mark for each valid comparison to a maximum of 3 marks.*

Responses could include:

Third		Public		Private
increase donations	whereas	use tax payers money efficiently	whereas	increase profits
attract more volunteers		meet government targets		satisfy shareholders
be socially responsible				
provide a good service				
have a good image				

(b) (i) *Outline at least 1 cost and 1 benefit to a maximum of 4 marks. 1 mark for each valid point, up to 2 marks for any one cost or benefit, maximum 3 marks for either costs or benefits.*
Responses could include:
Costs
- Financial cost of training course/expensive to run.
- Loss of production.
  ◦ Loss of sales revenue.
- Staff may demand higher wages.
- Staff may leave for better paid jobs.

Benefits
- Increased flexibility.
  ◦ Employees could cover for absentees.
- Employees more productive.
- Improved quality of work.
- Less wastage/accidents.
- Increased job satisfaction.
- Improved customer service/satisfaction.

(ii) *State at least 2 methods to a maximum of 4 marks. 1 mark for each valid method, up to 3 marks for any one method. Maximum 3 marks for payment methods.*
Responses could include:
- Provide flexible working hours.
  ◦ By allowing employees to choose start and finishing times.
- Provide permanent contracts.
  ◦ So the job lasts as long as the business operates.
- Pay a bonus.
  ◦ Which is an additional payment on top of normal salary.
- Pay a higher rate of pay for working overtime.
- Provide payment based on the amount of goods sold.

(c) *Explain at least 2 benefits to a maximum of 3 marks. 1 mark for each explained benefit, up to 2 marks for any one benefit.*
Responses could include:
- If location is close to customers – it gives them easy access.
- If the location has parking close by – this makes it easier for donations to be dropped off.
- If the location does not have a lot of competition nearby – sales are likely to increase.
- If location has low rent/purchase price – this will help to minimise costs of the business.
  ◦ Increasing funds available for the cause.

(d) (i) *Identify 2 types of technology for a maximum of 2 marks. 1 mark for each correctly identified use.*

Responses could include:
- (CHAS) website/online donating facilities/internet.
- Social media.

(ii) *1 mark for each valid description to a maximum of 3 marks. Up to 3 marks for any one use/piece of technology.*
Responses could include:
CHAS website/donating online facilities
- To make donating easier.
  ◦ Ease of donating may encourage repeat donations (loyalty).
- Will provide information.
  ◦ Based on this they may volunteer or attend an event.

Social media
- Can increase awareness of the charity.
- Specific markets can be targeted.
- Can be used for advertising 24/7.

Software/ IT Packages
- Word-processing packages can be used to create company logo.
- Database can be used to keep previous donor's details to target when trying to raise donations.
- Spreadsheets can be used to keep sales information.
  ◦ Charts can be produced to analyse trends in sales.

Email
- Can be used to contact stakeholders over a wide geographical area.

Accept also:
- Reputation of organisation for being up to date with technology.
- Large amounts of finance will need to be invested to purchase technology.
- Staff will need to be trained.

Section 2

3. (a) *1 mark for each valid description to a maximum of 3 marks. Up to 3 marks for any one description.*
Responses could include:
- Identifies consumer needs/wants.
  ◦ Ensures the product has a chance of success.
  ◦ Allows you to set an appropriate selling price.
- Identifies the target market.
  ◦ Can promote products specifically to its target market.
- Gains information on consumer trends/behaviour.
  ◦ Allows the organisation to cope more effectively with changes in trends.
- Gains information on rivals/competition.
  ◦ Allows the organisation to replicate or get ideas from competitors.

(b) *Outline at least 2 stages to a maximum of 4 marks. 1 mark for each outlined stage, up to 3 marks for any one stage.*
Responses could include:
- Carry out market research.
- Generate the idea.
  ◦ Brainstorming session or focus group.
- Analyse the idea.
- Produce a prototype.
  ◦ Create a model of the product.
- Test the product.
  ◦ E.g. safety, durability tests etc.

- ◦ Receive feedback from test market on how to improve.
- Adjust the product based on tests and feedback.
  - ◦ Change the packaging.
- Produce the product.
- Decide on the advertising and promotions/ advertise so consumers know it is available.

(c) *2 benefits to a maximum of 3 marks. 1 mark for each valid description, up to 2 marks for any one benefit.*
Responses could include:
- Brands are instantly recognisable — saves finance on advertising.
  - ◦ Gives a higher market share.
- Branding can enable a business to charge high prices for its product — can make larger profits.
- Branding can lead to a perception of high quality — can charge high prices.
- Branding can lead to brand loyalty — customers are likely to make repeat purchases.
- Easier to launch new products — as already gained trust.

4. (a) *Describe at least 2 methods to a maximum of 4 marks. 1 mark for each description, up to 3 marks for any one method.*
Responses could include:
Quality Control
- Quality is checked at the beginning (inputs)/end (outputs) of the production process.
  - ◦ Unacceptable products are either scrapped or put back for reworking.

Quality Assurance
- Quality is checked at every stage of the production process.

Quality Inputs
- Ensuring that raw materials are the best that they can be to ensure a quality output.
- Ensuring that machinery/equipment is up-to-date.
  - ◦ Fully maintained so that it is working to its best at all times.
- Ensuring the recruitment process gets the best staff.
- Training staff to ensure they can produce to the best quality.

(b) *Outline at least 2 factors to a maximum of 3 marks. 1 mark for each outlined factor, up to 2 marks for any one factor. Quality of product should be qualified.*
Responses could include:
- The nature of the product.
- An individual product made to order/standardised.
- The number of customers wanting to buy the product.
- The availability and skills of labour.
- If there is cheap labour in an area.
- The availability of technology/machinery.
- The cost of technology/machinery.
- The finance available.
- The size of the premises.

(c) *Explain at least 2 impacts to a maximum of 3 marks. 1 mark for each impact, up to 2 marks for any one impact.*
Responses could include:
- Goods may deteriorate — which could lead to high wastage costs.
- Greater chance of theft — as it is more difficult to notice if something is missing.
  - ◦ Which would mean loss of profit from stolen goods.

- Greater storage/insurance costs — which could mean prices may need to rise.
- Goods may become obsolete — which wastes resources as no-one is willing to buy.
- Capital is tied up in inventory — which means that resources cannot be used elsewhere.
- More storage space is required — which leaves less space available for production.
- Organisation is able to immediately respond to surge in demand — which would increase sales.

5. (a) *Identify 2 pieces of legislation for a maximum of 2 marks. 1 mark for each identified piece of legislation. Year is not required. No abbreviations or the Freedom of Information Act.*
Responses could include:
- Equality Act.
- Health & Safety at Work Act.
- National Minimum Wage.
- National Living Wage.

(b) (i) *Identify 2 methods for a maximum of 2 marks. 1 mark for each identified method.*
Responses could include:
- Application form/CV.
- Interview.
- References.
- Testing.

(ii) *Explain one benefit of each method to a maximum of 2 marks. 1 mark for each explained benefit.*
Responses could include:
Application form/CV
- To compare against the job description and person specification — in order to narrow down the list of potential candidates/create a short list.
- To see if candidate has the necessary qualifications/experience — so that training costs can be reduced.

Interviews
- Candidates are asked a set of identical questions — which will allow the organisation to compare each candidate.
- Candidate can be asked questions relating to their application form — to see if they can back up what they said.

References
- Candidate's past performance in a work situation can be known — which will help back-up their personal statement.

Testing
- Assessing a candidate's performance — to see if they can work under pressure.

(c) *1 mark for each valid effect to a maximum of 4 marks. Up to 4 marks for any one effect.*
Responses could include:
- Production will stop/slow down.
- The firm gains a bad image.
  - ◦ This may put customers off buying from the company in the future.
- Employees' morale falls.
  - ◦ Could lead to higher staff turnover.
- Expenses may increase if conditions are met.
- Employees may lose income whilst taking strike action.

6. (a) *At least one advantage and one disadvantage to a maximum of 4 marks. 1 mark for any advantage/disadvantage, up to 3 marks for any one advantage/disadvantage.*
Responses could include:
Advantages
- Increased finance through shareholders and lenders.
- Shareholders have limited liability.
  ∘ Their personal possessions are not at risk if the organisation goes into debt.
- Control of the company is not lost to outsiders.
  ∘ All shareholders have to be agreed upon and invited to invest.
- Financial risk is spread between the shareholders.
- Directors and shareholders expertise and experience can be called upon.

Disadvantages
- Decision making more complex as there could be many shareholders.
  ∘ Potential disagreements between shareholders.
- Profits will be shared (between shareholders).
- Shares cannot be sold to the general public.
  ∘ Reducing the capacity to raise finance.
- A legal process must be followed when setting up.
  ∘ Must comply with the Companies Act.
- Annual accounts must be produced.

(b) *Describe the influence of at least 2 stakeholders to a maximum of 4 marks. 1 mark for each valid description, up to 3 marks for any one influence.*
Responses could include:
Managers
- Through the decisions they make.
- By motivating staff.
  ∘ Increases productivity.

Employees
- Through the standard of their work.
- Through different forms of industrial action (such as a strike).

Shareholders
- Through their voting rights at the AGM.
- Through the level of investment made/withdrawn.

Bank/Lenders
- By choosing to approve/not approve loan applications.
- Through the setting of interest rates.
- Through pay-back conditions.

Suppliers
- By offering trade credit.
- Increasing/decreasing prices.
- Level of discounts offered.
- Timely delivery.

Customers
- By choosing to buy/not to buy from an organisation.
- Through positive/negative word-of-mouth.

Local Community
- By petitioning and making complaints to the local council.

Pressure Groups
- By carrying out negative advertising/demonstrations.

Government
- Could change taxation levels.
- Could increase National Minimum Wage/National Living Wage.
- Could change/introduce legislation.

(c) *1 mark for each valid identification to a maximum of 2 marks.*
Responses could include:
- (Availability/skills of) employees.
- (Skills of) managers.
- (Availability of) finance.
- (Availability of) technology.

7. (a) *Calculate all 3 missing figures to a maximum of 3 marks. 1 mark for each correctly calculated figure.*
Responses should include:
 (i) £1,000
 (ii) £5,000
 (iii) £6,000

(b) *Describe at least 2 uses of technology to a maximum of 4 marks. 1 mark for each valid description, up to 3 marks for any one use.*
Responses could include:
Spreadsheets
- Creation of financial documents (max 1).
  ∘ Formulae can be used to help do calculations.
  ∘ This reduces chance of errors.
- Could be used to display financial information in graphical/chart form.

Word processing
- Could be used to create invoices to send to customers requesting payment.

Database
- Could be used to record supplier/customer information.
- Could be used to create reports on customers with overdue accounts.

Presentation software
- Could be used to deliver a presentation displaying financial information.

Internet
- Could be used to check customer credit ratings.

E-mail
- Could be used to remind customers when their payments are due.

(c) *Define all 3 terms to a maximum of 3 marks. 1 mark for each valid definition.*
Responses could include:
Expenses
- Costs/overheads incurred by the business.
- Money spent by the business e.g. rent (*needs e.g.*).

Profit for the Year
- Profit made after expenses have been deducted/gross profit less expenses.

Gross Profit
- Profit made from buying and selling inventory/sales revenue less cost of sales.

Acknowledgements

Permission has been sought from all relevant copyright holders and Hodder Gibson is grateful for the use of the following:

An extract and logo from www.justdogsshop.co.uk © Just Dogs (2016 page 2);
Logo © Who Made Your Pants/Becky John (2016 page 3);
An article and photo about Charles Macleod Stornoway Black Pudding. Reproduced by permission of Charles Macleod Ltd (2017 page 2);
Image © margo555/stock.adobe.com (2017 page 3);
Information and logo taken from www.iqchoc.com. Reproduced by kind permission of iQ Superfood Chocolate (2017 page 3);
Information and logo reproduced by kind permission of Cuddybridge Apple Juice (www.cuddybridgeapplejuice.com) (2017 SQP page 2);
Infographic from 'Tetra Pak® 2016 Juice Index Report' and statistics from Mintel GNPD 2015 (Vegetable Nutrition), Tetra Pak consumer survey (All Natural) and Roper Reports Worldwide 2015 (Speciality 100% Juice). Reproduced by permission of Tetra Pak (2017 SQP page 2);
Infographic from 'Changing Tastes: The UK Soft Drinks Annual Report 2015' © The British Soft Drinks Association and statistics from Zenith International (2017 SQP page 2);
A passage adapted from www.fifteen.net © Jamie Oliver Food Foundation (2017 SQP page 4);
Image © Yui Mok/PA Archive/PA Images (2017 SQP page 4);
A logo and extract from 'Channel4Dispatches — Supermarkets: Brexit & Your Shrinking Shop' © Channel 4 TV (2017 SQP page 4);
Logo and information taken from www.hellofresh.co.uk are reproduced by permission of HelloFresh (2018 page 2);
Logo and information taken from www.chas.org.uk are reproduced by permission of CHAS (2018 page 4);
UK charities' statistics are reproduced by permission of nfpSynergy (2018 page 4).